The Anger Overload Workbook For Children and Teens

Take Charge of Your Anger

By David Gottlieb, Ph.D.
and Shira Gottlieb, Psy.D.

The Anger Overload Workbook

Table of Contents

Preface: Note to coaches   4

Section 1: Understanding your triggers

Chapter 1: Taking charge of your anger   7

Chapter 2: Pick a coach   9

Chapter 3: When do you get angry?   10

Section 2: Preventing anger

Chapter 4: Avoid the situation or alter your routine   17

Chapter 5: How to use a mantra   19

Section 3: What to do for low levels of anger

Chapter 6: Low versus high levels of anger   22

Chapter 7: Becoming aware of body signals   25

Chapter 8: Calming activities that use emotional distraction   28

Section 4: What to do for high levels of anger

Chapter 9: Picking a "go to place"   35

Chapter 10: Review and practice   37

Section 5: More advanced techniques

Chapter 11: How to deal with different points of view   41

Chapter 12: How to compromise   45

Chapter 13: How to verbalize anger without losing self-control   49

Drs. David and Shira Gottlieb

Section 6: Conclusion

Chapter 14: Ongoing review of anger plan — 52

Chapter 15: Summary — 53

Appendix: Extra set of worksheets for your coach — 54

Acknowledgements:
We would like to acknowledge Loring Ingraham, Ph.D., Terrence Koller, Ph.D., and Mark Reinecke, Ph.D. for reading over our manuscript and making helpful suggestions. Thanks also to Fawn Gottlieb and David Hampton for their help editing the book.

© Copyright 2016 by David and Shira Gottlieb

The Anger Overload Workbook

Preface: Note to coaches

The child or teen whom you will be coaching is about to begin a path toward better controlling his or her anger. (We will hereafter usually refer to "children," not teens, but the workbook is designed for children and teens from age 8 to 18. Also, we will generally use the pronoun "his," but the workbook is designed for use by boys and girls.) Developing better control of one's anger will lead to more satisfying relationships throughout the child's life. With new self-control, he will be able to communicate his feelings without scaring or alienating people. The workbook explains strategies to help him, and as a coach you will be supporting him through this process.

It is generally a good idea to read the workbook together and assist as needed with the worksheets. For young children, you may need to read the chapters out loud if the children are not yet able to read them. Older teens may prefer to read and fill out the worksheets by themselves.

We recommend concentrating on one chapter for a week. If you rush through the manual, the child is less likely to remember what he has worked on. Also, you don't want the workbook to become a burden. There are several places in the workbook where we recommend taking more than a week to practice some of the skills. There will be a picture of a policeman holding up a stop sign where we suggest you take more time to review the strategies together.

Sometimes you will be asked to share some experiences of your own. We all struggle at times with anger, and it is important that you show the child that you are working on it, too. You want him to see that he is not alone in dealing with anger. You will help serve as a role model at times in this workbook.

At other times, you will be asked to help the child remember how he reacted in a situation, if he forgets, and if you were there to observe what happened. Please encourage the child to write down some of his experiences in what we call his "anger diary." The anger diary is what the child records on the four worksheets in the first section of the book. These first four worksheets help identify each person's anger triggers. You both will refer to this diary as you proceed through the workbook. Keep in mind that the child is ultimately in control of what he writes down in his anger diary and in the workbook exercises. If he disagrees with your memory of the events, let him be in charge.

Be encouraging. When you see the child working hard on the exercises, let him know what a good job he is doing. Also, be understanding when things get difficult. This is not an easy process, and some days the child may get discouraged or have trouble with the workbook exercises. At these times, empathize with how frustrating some of the work can be. Use your judgment about whether to encourage him to keep trying, or whether to suggest a break if he seems too frustrated or stuck. Or, if he will let you help with a difficult section, then you could make suggestions, or even do some of the writing for him. If the latter, be sure to review your ideas with him before writing in his workbook. It is important that the child "owns" what is written, that he feels it is an accurate description of what goes through his mind. If you impose your ideas on a child who is not really in agreement, then he will be less likely to learn and change his behavior. Go slowly, and take breaks as needed.

If a child does not want to work on the exercises, think about why. Does he feel embarrassed, or does he feel criticized, or is he in denial about his anger issues? This would be a good time to share some of your own experiences with anger in order to help "normalize" how anger can be "messy," that is, to show how it can get out of control for most of us. If the child feels frustrated and says that it is impossible to control his anger, then share if you ever felt this way about your anger or some other emotion at some point in your life. Explain that children (let alone adults) are not supposed to be able to control their emotions all the time. It takes time and practice.

I also want to emphasize that the goal is improvement in self-control, not perfect self-control. This means that a child can be making progress, but still lose control sometimes. Also, self-control does not mean that a child must calmly explain his feelings or disagree without raising his voice at all. While this would be wonderful, anger is an emotion that is not easily expressed in a calm manner. It is within acceptable limits if a child raises his voice and argues when he is mad. This is not anger overload. Overload occurs when a child uses words or actions that show total disregard and disrespect for other people. Therefore, the goal is to reduce outbursts that go beyond arguing to swearing, calling people hurtful names, becoming physically aggressive toward other people, or destroying objects of importance to others.

Throughout the workbook, remember the importance of **empathy**. Be understanding about how hard it can be to keep anger from getting out of control. Help the child adjust his expectations so as not to expect changes overnight. It can take months to work through all the exercises, and it can take months to see improvement in self-control.

If a child does not like the ideas in one of the chapters, then it is okay to move on to another chapter. There are many chapters with various strategies, and it is not necessary to use them all. If he wants to take a break, think about why that might be, and empathize with how he is feeling. Remember that you do not want the workbook to become a source of conflict between you and him.

You will see that the workbook is divided into six main sections. First is "understanding your anger": in this section, the child will be instructed on how to keep a brief anger diary. The next section (section 2) is about "preventing anger" to be followed by "what to do for low levels of anger" (section 3). If a child can prevent a potentially upsetting situation from arising or if he can catch his anger early, it will be easier for him to control it. This is not always possible, so the next section (section 4) is about "what to do for high levels of anger." Then for older children and teens, the 5th section has "more advanced techniques." Finally, section 6 explains the importance of ongoing practice and review of the child's anger plan.

In the back of the workbook is the appendix with extra worksheets that you as the coach can use for showing the child how you deal with angry feelings. At several points during the workbook, you will be asked to fill out a form from the appendix. Please do this and show the child. In this way, you serve as an important role model that will help the child to work on his anger.

Thanks for agreeing to be the child's coach. You are an important part of the process. Be sure to pat yourself on the back from time to time, as well as the child! And don't forget to celebrate your work together, especially after completing each of the five main sections of the workbook. The exercises in the anger overload workbook can be hard work. So be sure to reflect on the progress the child is making, and celebrate periodically with an activity that is fun for you both.

Drs. David and Shira Gottlieb

Section 1: Understanding your triggers

Chapter 1: Taking charge of your anger

Do you sometimes let loose with your anger on someone you care about? Do you later wish you could have reacted a little differently? Some people swear or say that they hate someone when they are mad, and later feel badly because they really care about the person they got mad at. Other people strike something or someone when they are angry, but regret it when they calm down. This book will help you get control of your anger. You will still let people know when they do something you do not like, but you won't lash out. You may still raise your voice and argue sometimes, but you will be able to stop before you swear or say horrible things about another person, and before you become physical and harm someone or something.

Anger overload is the term we use for when anger gets out of our control, for when our anger takes over. Most of the time we are calm and easy to get along with. But when we get angry, we sometimes get really revved up and say whatever comes to our mind. It may only last a few minutes, usually less than an hour. But during that time, we say or do things that we often later regret.

How does this happen? Deep inside our brains is an area (called the amygdala) that gets activated when we get angry. It sends signals to our outer brain (called the cerebral cortex) that is the control center that helps us decide what to say or do. When we say or do things in anger that hurt other people, the cerebral cortex is not exercising control. Scientists are not exactly sure what is happening inside the cortex of our brains, but we do know that when we work on developing self-control, our brain centers become more developed. It's similar to what happens when you exercise your leg or arm muscles. Your body gets stronger.

Anger usually gets triggered when something does not work out the way we expected. We get frustrated. Someone may disappoint or ignore us. They may not do what we thought they were going to do for us. Or they may criticize us. Or even threaten us physically. The threats or frustrations that arouse our anger are usually unexpected and can affect us deeply. We call the threats, criticisms, disappointments, or frustrations "triggers." In the pages that follow, you will see that the first step toward taking charge of your anger is noticing what a few of those triggers are: What do other people do or say that gets you angry? And who is it that you get angry at more often?

It is important to try to take charge of your anger because if you explode at someone, that person will not want to listen to your side of the story. The person will be upset with you for exploding rather than be interested in why you got upset. They will react negatively to the way you behaved.

Think about it. If someone calls you a swear word, would you think about the other person's feelings, or would you just react to being called an awful word? To get people to listen to you, you can't blow them out of the water. It is okay to get angry, but you need to clearly state what is bothering you, and it is hard to be clear if your anger is over the top.

Another problem with calling people mean names or striking out at them is that it may cause them to stay away from you in the future. While your family will likely forgive you, other people may not. Your friends may stop hanging around you for fear that you will let loose on them again. Even if you don't mean any harm, and even if you are usually nice to other people, they will not be so quick to forget your outbursts. It is important to learn how to take charge of your anger now, before you do harm to your relationships. This book will help you gain control.

There are exceptions when extreme reactions are called for, such as when someone threatens your physical safety. But for most people this rarely, if ever, occurs. More likely is someone putting you down, or stopping you from doing something you were planning on doing. If you react by throwing something at someone else, what will they think of you?

Before we get started, remember that no one does this perfectly. Most of us can lose it sometimes. The goal is to have self-control most of the time. That way people will listen better to what you have to say, and they will respect you. In addition, you will feel proud of yourself that you have become the boss of your anger, rather than letting your anger get the best of you.

Drs. David and Shira Gottlieb

Chapter 2: Pick a coach

You are beginning an important journey. You are going to learn how to take charge of your anger so you won't regret later what you said or did. You get along with your family and friends most all the time. But when something gets under your skin, you sometimes say something or do something that hurts other people. There are usually good reasons why you got mad. Somebody may have ignored you, or someone may have stopped you from doing something you wanted to do, or someone may have criticized you. This first step is keeping track of some of those situations when you get mad. What happens before you get really angry?

Before you get started, find someone to be your coach. When you learn anything new, whether it is learning to be a better hitter in baseball or to play a musical instrument, it helps to have a coach. Even professional baseball players have batting coaches who can point out things about their swing, or give tips on how to hit a curve ball.

Think about whom you trust to be your coach. You want someone who has time to work with you, who has good ideas, and who has patience. What about the adult who gave you this workbook? Does he or she tend to give good advice without being too critical of you? You want someone who will not get too mad at you if you have a rough day.

You also want a coach who can admit that he or she gets angry sometimes and who can share with you what happened. Your coach does not have to have all the answers about how to handle angry outbursts. He does not have to be perfect and always have control of his anger. But you want a coach who usually can handle his anger without totally losing it. Because your coach has had experience dealing with his own anger, he will have some tips that may be useful for you.

So ask the person whom you are considering to be your coach to tell you about a time he lost his cool. What got him mad, and what did he do that he wishes he had not said or done? Also ask if the situation happened again, what would he do (or what did he do) to handle it differently? After listening to your potential coach, do you feel he or she could be of help to you? Has he worked on anger himself, and do you feel he could understand what you are going through? Then ask him to be your coach. Remember if it doesn't work out you can always change coaches.

The Anger Overload Workbook

Chapter 3: When do you get angry?

Creating an anger diary

The first step toward taking charge of your anger is to figure out what triggers your anger? **What** sometimes gets you mad and **whom** do you sometimes get mad at? Think about a time you got angry in the last few weeks. What did someone say or do that got you angry, and what did you say or do then? Fill in your answers below. You don't have to worry about spelling or writing long sentences. This is for you to keep track. You are not going to turn it in at school. Just write a few words so that you will be able to look back later and remember what got you angry.

The person you got angry at _____

What this person said or did that made you mad
_____
_____

What you said or did when you felt angry
_____
_____

After you got mad, where did you go until you felt better?
_____

What did you do until you felt better?_____

You just took an important step. Before you can take charge of your anger, you need to see when it happens. Not everyone is ready to keep a record. To do this, you have to think back about what happened in the last few weeks. Some people have trouble remembering, and some people aren't ready to admit that anything gets them mad. If you have trouble remembering, don't worry. Sometimes it is hard to remember things. The next time you get mad, try to jot down your answers right after you calm down. Or see if your coach can help you get started. Sometimes if someone helps you remember, it will all come back to you, and you will then be able to write it down.

Remember everyone gets mad sometimes. Some things make us furious, and once you see what some of those things are, you will be able to be take charge of your anger. This book will help you learn to control your anger, rather than have your anger control you.

One other thing to do at this time: Ask your coach to write down a time in the last few weeks when he or she got angry. Have your coach answer these questions for himself:

Drs. David and Shira Gottlieb

The person you got angry at _____

What this person said or did that made you mad
_____
_____

What you said or did when you felt angry
_____
_____

After you got mad, where did you go until you felt better?
_____

What did you do until you felt better? _____

    Keeping a record or "diary" is such a key part of learning how to control anger that we want you to write down several more situations that get you mad in the next few weeks. Use worksheet #1 below. Don't try to answer the questions while you are angry. Wait until you feel calmer and then jot down whom you were angry with and what they said or did that got you angry. Your coach can help you remember some details if you want.

    Try to write your observations the same day you get angry so you will be more likely to remember. If you forget some of the details, don't worry about it. See if your coach remembers, or else leave one or more of the questions in the chart blank, and then wait until the next time you get angry before writing again. There is space to record up to five times when you get mad in the next few weeks. (You can use what you wrote down at the beginning of this chapter for one of your five entries in worksheet #1.) There are more copies in the back of this book for your coach. Have your coach also answer the questions for when he or she gets angry in the next few weeks.

My Anger Diary: Worksheet #1

1. The person you got angry at _____

What this person said or did that made you mad
_____
_____

What you said or did when you felt angry
_____
_____

After you got mad, where did you go until you felt better?
_____

The Anger Overload Workbook

What did you do until you felt better? _____

2. The person you got angry at _____

What this person said or did that made you mad
_____
_____

What you said or did when you felt angry
_____
_____

After you got mad, where did you go until you felt better?
_____

What did you do until you felt better? _____

3. The person you got angry at _____

What this person said or did that made you mad
_____
_____

What you said or did when you felt angry
_____
_____

After you got mad, where did you go until you felt better?
_____

What did you do until you felt better? _____

4. The person you got angry at _____

What this person said or did that made you mad
_____
_____

Drs. David and Shira Gottlieb

What you said or did when you felt angry
_____
_____

After you got mad, where did you go until you felt better?
_____

What did you do until you felt better?_____

5. The person you got angry at _____

What this person said or did that made you mad
_____
_____

What you said or did when you felt angry
_____
_____

After you got mad, where did you go until you felt better?
_____

What did you do until you felt better?_____

Wait three or more weeks or until you and your coach have jotted down some times you each got angry.

The Anger Overload Workbook

Look for patterns: Did something happen more than once?

Now that you and your coach have written down some examples of when you got angry during the last few weeks, and what you did, look back at what you wrote and see if some of the situations are similar. Finding patterns is an important step in your effort to control your anger. All the situations won't fit into one or two types. But if you can find some similarities, then that will give you clues about your anger.

Looking for patterns: Worksheet #2

Are you usually mad at certain people? _____

And do you usually say certain words or do certain things when you get mad?
_____
_____

Lastly, where do you usually go and what do you do while you are calming down?
_____
_____

Now let's look more closely at the people and situations that get you angry. First look at whom you tend to get mad at. Circle any of the people below whom you have been angry with in the last few weeks.

Identifying Who and What Gets You Mad: Worksheet #3

A. People you get mad at:

1. Your mother
2. Your father
3. Your brother
4. Your sister
5. Your teacher
6. Your friend
7. Yourself
8. _____

Now look over your diary and think about what these people say or do that gets you mad. How do they sometimes frustrate you? Here are some choices that might fit for you, but if you see another pattern that fits better for you, then write that in the blank space below. Circle any of the triggers below that fit for your anger.

Drs. David and Shira Gottlieb

B. What these people said or did that got you mad:

1. They didn't let you do what you wanted.
2. They did something that was unfair.
3. They criticized you.
4. They ignored you.
5. They made you do something that you didn't want to do.
6. They interrupted what you were doing.
7. You got mad at yourself when you made a mistake.
8. _____

Let's see if you can add more details to what it was that angered you. Below are some questions for each of the above triggers. Look for the number(s) of the triggers you just circled and then read the questions for those types of triggers below. Write in your answers in the spaces provided.

Pinning down what happened to you: Worksheet #4

Look for the triggers you just circled in worksheet # 3:

#1 If they didn't let you do what you wanted:

Is it usually an activity at home or out of the house? _____

Do you want to play a game or use an electronic device? Or do you want to spend more time with friends? Or is it something else you want to do?
_____

#2: If they were unfair:

Which situation are they more likely to be unfair about:

a) when you want to do something that your brothers, sisters, or friends are allowed to do, but you aren't, or

b) when you want to do something else that you think is reasonable but they don't?

What is it you want to do? _____

#3: If you were criticized:

Are you criticized by friends or adults? _____

The Anger Overload Workbook

Is it because of something they think you did wrong, or is someone picking on you because you are different in some way, like the way you dress or talk?
_____

#4: If you felt ignored:

Think about if there are certain times that this is more likely to happen: Is it at home or at school?
_____

If it is at home, is it usually after dinner, before bedtime, or when you ask for something? _____

If it is at school, is it in class, at free time, or at lunch?
_____

#5: If you were made to do things you did not want to do:

Is the issue about chores, homework, getting ready for bed, or something else?
_____

#6: If they interrupted what you were doing:

When is this more likely to happen: while you are on the computer, playing a game, watching television, or something else?
_____

#7: If you got mad at yourself when you made a mistake:

Is it a mistake on schoolwork or homework, or does it have to do with an electronic game, a competitive sports game, or something else?
_____

#8: If it was a different trigger:

What else are you doing when you get mad?
_____

Now you are ready for the first strategy to help you be the boss of your anger.

Drs. David and Shira Gottlieb

Section 2: Preventing anger

Chapter 4: Avoid the situation or alter your routine

Now that you have determined some situations that get you angry, one approach to preventing anger overload is to **avoid** these situations, if possible. For example if the problem has to do with trigger number 3 (you get criticized), you may be able to avoid the trigger. If there is a person who sometimes criticizes you, can you stay away from this person, or at least avoid them when they seem like they might be in a crabby mood? If you can avoid the situation, then you prevent your anger from being triggered.

Similarly, if the problem is that you get mad at yourself when you make a mistake (trigger number 7), think about which activity triggers this reaction in yourself. It may be a particular type of game that you expect yourself to do well at, and when you don't do well, you get so mad that you throw something at the wall, or scream swear words. Maybe this only happens when you are tired or when you are already stressed out. Then avoid the activity at these times, and you will prevent anger overload. Of course, there are some activities you can't avoid or don't want to avoid, and then you will need another strategy.

Some triggers you cannot avoid even if you want to: for example, the problem may occur when your parents insist that you do something. You probably won't be able to get them to stop requesting you do things, like chores or homework. But maybe you will be able to talk with them when everyone is calm about how to take some pressure off you. Ask your coach how you might approach this with your parent(s). If your coach is your parent, then ask him or her if there is a way to alter the task in some way, maybe by changing the time when you have to do things.

Another possible solution would be for you and your parent to establish a reminder system so that your parent won't have to nag you to do a chore. One example would be to put a post-it-note on your bedroom door or on the refrigerator. This will help you remember what you need to do. Hopefully this reminder will lead to your doing the chore before you and your parents get angry with each other.

If you shift the time or establish a new reminder system, you are **altering your routine** in order to prevent anger overload. You still have to do what your parents ask, but you try to arrange the schedule or the reminder system to lessen the chance for conflict.

Altering your routine may work for several sources of your anger. It can apply to some of the triggers listed in the last worksheet, such as number 1 (They didn't let you do what you wanted.), number 5 (They made you do something that you didn't want to do.), and number 6 (They interrupted what you were doing.). Let's look more closely at one of these triggers: if you indicated that the problem has to do with your parents not letting you spend time on the computer or with your friends (trigger number 1), think about why that is. Maybe they don't object to your having fun, but just want you do something else first. For example, it is not unusual that some children and teens want a break after school to go online, but some parents say no because they want their child to do his homework. Is there a way to compromise? Can you alter your routine so that your parents do not worry about you doing your homework, but so that you get some time on the computer? One suggestion you could make is that you will do part of your homework first and then take a break.

Think about whether there is a way you could alter the routine for any of the triggers you described in the previous chapter. Could you change the time you do something, or could you think of a good way to remind yourself so that your parents will not have to nag you? Write a possible alternative in the worksheet below, and later when the person you get mad at is relaxed and not busy, show him what you are thinking. If the person will not change his mind, think about some other way you might alter your routine that may be more agreeable to everyone. If you can find a way to alter your routine, you may be able to prevent anger overload. If there is no way to do this, do not worry. We have just begun the search for strategies.

Can you alter your routine? Worksheet #5

1. What is one trigger you noted in the previous chapter?
___

Can you avoid the person or the activity?
___

Can you change the time you do the activity?
___

Is there a good way to remind yourself to do something that will satisfy the other person?
___

2. What is another trigger you noted in the previous chapter?
___

Can you avoid the person or the activity?
___

Can you change the time you do the activity?
___

Is there a good way to remind yourself to do something that will satisfy the other person?
___

Chapter 5: How to use a mantra

A mantra is a short, memorable saying that you can say, sing, or hum to yourself. Do you ever find yourself humming a line over and over again from one of your favorite songs or from a television commercial? Those catchy words are what we call a mantra. Here we are going to help you come up with mantras for situations that make you angry. The mantras will help you look at the situations in a new way. They will help you control your anger. You try to pick some words that are catchy, words that you are likely to remember. Then you will remind yourself every day what the mantra is. The more you practice thinking it to yourself, the more it will help you when something happens that bothers you. It will help your mood stay calm.

The best time to say the mantra to yourself is before you start something that has caused you frustration in the past. If you wait until you are already angry, it will be less effective. Try to get yourself in the right mindset just before you start something that has caused you stress in the past. It is important therefore to look over the triggers you wrote about in your anger diary (worksheets # 1-4) so that you can plan ahead.

Here is an example to show you what a mantra is and how it can help. If you get annoyed playing a video game because you lose your life and have to start over, you might get pretty angry. But if you think of a mantra before you start the game, you might not get so angry. The mantra could be "these games are made to be hard," or "the game makers want me to lose so I will keep playing the game over and over till I win." A mantra is a way to think about the situation differently. Instead of thinking "I've got to win this time" you think "the game is made so that I will eventually lose my life." In this way, you are prepared for losing. Mantras are true sayings. In other words, it is not making up a lie to make you feel better. Mantras reflect what is realistic and true about something.

When you are playing a video game, or engaged in some other competitive activity, you are trying so hard to win that you do not think about how the game was made to make people lose, you just think about beating it. You are so focused on winning that you get aggravated when you don't. So if you think about a mantra ahead of time before you start the game, it may help you keep in mind the truth about video games, about how they are designed to make you lose. Then you may not get so angry when you do lose because you know it is going to happen.

Another situation where a mantra can help ease frustration is when you have to take a test in school or when you have a difficult homework assignment. You may get aggravated with yourself when you can't figure something out, or when your parent reviews your homework and finds several mistakes. If you are trying hard to get every answer correct, then you may get very frustrated when you make a mistake. But if you come up with a mantra, it could help you stay on an even keel. Some possible mantras are "everyone makes mistakes" or "it's good to make some mistakes because it shows I'm learning something new." If you sometimes get angry when you make mistakes, you could try one of these mantras before you start your homework or test. If you'd prefer, think of another saying that will help you not worry so much about mistakes. You want the mantra to be something that makes sense to you and that you will remember. Then use it each day before you start your homework or before you take a test.

What if you get criticized or ignored? Then a possible mantra could be one of the following: "who cares what they think," "something must be bothering them today," or "I'm not going to let them ruin my day." The idea here is to not get too wrapped up in what other people think or say. It is important to realize that other people have bad days or problems, and that may be why they said something mean or why they ignored you. Maybe your friend was yelled at by her parents before she left for school, and she is taking it out on you. Or maybe she was teased by her brother or sister. Or maybe she is jealous of you. So don't take what she says seriously. What she says about you is not who you really are; it just reflects her crabby mood or her jealousy.

Look back at your anger diary, and have your coach look back at his. Pick one or two situations to start and think about why you got upset. Is there some other way to look at the situation that may help you get less aggravated? Fill out the worksheet below with one or two mantras.

It is hardest to come up with mantras for situations when you feel you were treated unfairly. It's hard because you may not see any reason for someone to treat you the way he/she did. You may not see another way of looking at the situation. Try to put yourself in the other person's shoes, and imagine how the other person might have been thinking: Why did he/she act this way? Was he trying to be unfair, or did he not realize it? What was he concerned about? What might have been on his mind? You may not agree that the person's concerns were valid or important, but can you see how he might have been thinking? We will work more on these questions in later chapters, so don't worry if you can't come up with a good mantra right now for when someone is being unfair to you.

Coming up with a mantra: Worksheet # 6

What situation bothered you?
_____
_____

What is a mantra that could help you look at this situation in a new way?
_____

What's another situation that bothered you?
_____
_____

What is a mantra you could use?
_____

To make the mantra more memorable, try to hum or sing it to yourself. It's okay if you start to laugh when you sing it. Laughing will help you remember it, and also help you feel more relaxed. It's hard to laugh and be angry at the same time! Songs are easier to remember than just words, so if you can make it into a little "jingle" or song, you will remember it better. If songs don't work for you, then skip this idea. Maybe you are a more visual person. You could then draw a picture of the situation that bothers you, and write the mantra underneath the picture. Then put it in your room where you will see it. This will help you remember the mantra.

In order for a mantra to work well, it is important to practice it each day. Talk with your coach about a frustrating situation from the worksheet above, and then tell your coach what your mantra could be. If you practice saying your mantra out loud with your coach, you will be more likely to remember it if the frustrating situation happens again. Pick a convenient time each day to touch base with your coach and practice.

The more you practice, the more automatic it becomes to think about it before something bad happens, or to think about it right when something starts to frustrate you. After you have practiced for a couple of weeks, try to think about it right before something difficult or frustrating might happen. Look at the worksheet you filled out above to remind yourself of the situations when you could use a mantra. If you are playing a video game or going to be seeing a person who has sometimes frustrated you, say the mantra to yourself before you get together, or before you start the game. See if it helps you stay calm. Congratulate yourself if you remember to use the mantra, even if it doesn't work perfectly. You may still get upset, but try the mantra again for a few weeks. It probably will help sometimes. If not, change to a different mantra, or read the next section for other strategies you can use.

The Anger Overload Workbook

Section 3: What to do for low levels of anger

Chapter 6: Low versus high levels of anger

When you get angry do you sometimes get in such a rage that you swear, or scream about how much you hate someone, someone whom you really love? Or do you get physically angry and throw or kick things, or hit someone? This level of anger we call anger overload. Your brain has gotten overheated with angry feelings, and you let it out on someone you usually get along well with.

What do you say or do when you are in anger overload? Look back at your anger diary (worksheets # 1-4) and see what some of your behaviors are in a high anger state. Write down below (in worksheet # 7) what you say or do when you are in overload, that is, when your anger is extreme. Your coach can help you with this if you want, and also ask your coach to fill out his worksheet in the coach's section in the back of the book.

Now look at your diary again, and notice what you say or do when you are a little angry, but not to the max. For some children and teens, this might be raising their voice and being sarcastic, saying "Come on," "Really now," "I hate that," or "That's so unfair." Maybe you get into an intense argument when you are in the low anger stage. Notice that all these remarks stop short of swearing, calling people names, and throwing things. You can be mad without using words like "idiot" or "a-hole." Think about what you say when you are angry, but not totally disrespectful. What do you say or do then? Add an example or two to the worksheet below for when your anger is in the lower range.

Over the next few weeks, write down other examples of when you get extremely angry and write examples when your anger is at a lower level. It's important to distinguish these two levels, because what you do to take charge of your anger will be different depending on whether you are at a low level of anger or at anger overload. When you are in the low anger state, you can think more clearly and make choices about what to do.

We will explain to you in the next two chapters some strategies to gain control of your anger when it is low. You may already have some ideas in mind about what has worked when your anger is low. If you remember something you have done before that helped you feel in control of your anger, write it down in the worksheet below. If you are unsure, then leave it out.

When you are in the high anger state, you won't be thinking so clearly. You will be screaming or physically moving about (you may be even throwing or kicking). You will not be in the mood to think about what to do to control your anger. You will be letting it all out. What, if anything, has helped you to settle down in the past? Look over your anger diary to see if there is anything that has helped you in the high anger state.

One thing that helps many children and adults at both levels of anger is to go somewhere by themselves. Where can you be alone and calm down? It could be your bedroom, the family room, or the basement. It is hard to calm down when you are in the same room as the people who got you angry, because seeing them will stir up more anger most of the time. So think about a "go to place" for when you are angry, and we will look into what else you can do in future chapters.

For now, use the worksheet below to write down examples of your anger. Ask your coach to do the same in the back of the book for his anger over the next few weeks. Show each other your worksheets. Are there some similarities and some differences between you and your coach? Because your coach is older, he may have learned to control his anger most of the time, but maybe not. It does not matter whether most of the examples you and your coach write down are at high levels of anger, or at lower levels. Either way we will work on learning how to take charge of your anger in the next chapters of the workbook.

High and Low Anger: Worksheet # 7

What you do or say when **highly** angry:

1._____
_____

2._____
_____

3._____
_____

Anything that has helped when you were in a high anger state?
_____
_____
_____

What you do or say when your anger is **low:**

1._____
_____

2._____
_____

3._____
_____

Any ideas of what helped you control your anger?

Chapter 7: Becoming aware of body signals

Sometimes you can tell when you are likely to get angry because there are warning signs in your body. These signs are like a flashing yellow light that tells you there may be an anger outburst ahead. These warnings may not be obvious, but if you listen very carefully to your body's signals, you may notice some part of your body reacting right before you get really angry. Everyone's body is different, and everyone experiences different warning signs.

Let's look back at worksheets # 3 and 4 to remind yourself of who gets you mad and what they say or do that upsets you. The things people do or say that get you angry are called "triggers". Write down a few of the triggers in the worksheet below. Now be on the lookout for when one of these triggers occurs again, and then think about what is happening in your body.

Some of you may feel tightness or pain in your head, neck, shoulders or back. It may feel like your muscles are becoming tight like a rubber band that is ready to burst.

Other people tend to have reactions, like gas or cramps, in their stomach. People talk about feeling like there is tightness in their stomach. Other people feel their belly gurgling, and some get stomachaches. Do you have any of these feelings?

Some children and adults find that their breathing changes before they become angry. Your breath might become short and you might begin to breathe more quickly than you do when you are calm. Or, you might feel like you are holding your breath or not taking in enough air. Do you notice anything about your breathing before an anger outburst?

Other people feel their heart starting to beat faster; some people describe their heart as racing. Changes in your heart rate, your breathing, your stomach, or your neck or shoulders are possible as you begin to feel frustrated or angry. You may feel one or more of these things happen in your body.

This is your body's way of preparing to fight. This preparation is important if you are really in danger, but often our bodies prepare to fight when there is not any real danger around. If you have these feelings, there are ways to work on relaxing your body as a way of telling yourself "let's relax; it is not time to fight right now." At the end of this chapter, you will read about an exercise to help your body to relax. This strategy is called "rectangle" breathing, and it can help you release feelings of stress anywhere in your body. If you have these types of feelings, this exercise may be helpful for you.

Work with your coach to brainstorm possible warning signals you may experience before an anger outburst. Look at the triggers from your diary that you copied below, and think about whether your body acted up in a certain way. If you can't remember what your body felt like, that's okay. Wait until the next time you start feeling frustrated (you may feel annoyed or irritated with someone or with yourself), and then tell your coach about how your body feels, or write down anything you noticed in your body. Is there anything different you are feeling in your head, neck, back, stomach, heart, or breathing? If you don't feel like thinking about this when you are starting to get angry, then think about it afterward. Were there any warning signs?

Sometimes we get angry so fast that we don't have time to observe what our bodies are feeling. Don't get discouraged. If you notice some reactions in your body, write them down on the worksheet and use the exercises below. If you don't notice anything different in your body, then skip to the next chapter.

Knowing your body's signals: Worksheet # 8

What is one trigger for your anger?
_____

Are there any warning signs in your body? Circle any that apply to you, or write in one of your own.

a. Tightness or pain in your head, neck, back or shoulders
b. Stomach tightness, gurgling, or pain
c. Rapid breathing
d. Difficulty breathing
e. Heart beating faster
f. Other _____

What is another trigger for your anger? _____

Are there any warning signs in your body?
a. Tightness or pain in your head, neck, back or shoulders
b. Stomach tightness, gurgling, or pain
c. Rapid breathing
d. Difficulty breathing
e. Heart beating faster
f. Other _____

If you were able to observe some warning signs, continue reading. There is an exercise below that can help you become more aware of your body's signals and help you change these signals in order to send a new message: "to take it easy." If your body doesn't feel any different when you get mad, then skip to the next chapter.

"Mindfulness" exercise:

This experience of listening to how your body feels is called "mindfulness." The following mindfulness exercise will help you to listen to your body and help you to relax.

It takes some weeks of practice, but after you get experience with it, you will be able to calm yourself down much easier. We recommend you first practice when you are relaxing at home, like before bedtime. Then when you feel it working well for you, try it sometimes when you start to get frustrated. With practice, it will help you remain calm.

Mindfulness exercise:
This activity will focus on your breathing and help you to slow your breathing. When we breathe slowly with a long exhale we signal to our body that it is time to relax. We call this exercise "rectangle" breathing and you will soon see how it got this name.

- Find a rectangular object to focus on like a picture frame or a piece of paper.
- Breathe in through your nose slowly (like you are smelling flowers). While you breathe in, your eyes should follow the short side of the rectangle.
- Now breathe out through your mouth (like you are blowing out birthday candles). While you breathe out, your eyes should follow the long side of the rectangle.
- Continue this pattern as you go around the rectangle, breathing in for the short sides and out for the long sides.
- If you thoughts start to wander, or if you start to think about some issue that is bothering you, that's okay. Let the thoughts float away when they are ready.
- Then focus again on the rectangular object, and breathe in through your nose while your eyes follow the short side of the rectangle.
- And breathe out through your mouth as your eyes follow the long side of the rectangle.
- Practice this daily for about 30 seconds at first, and see if you can build up to one minute over the next two weeks.

Use other strategies as well:

In addition to the mindfulness exercise, you can use other strategies when your body tells you something is starting to bother you. Use one of the mantras you developed in the previous section of this workbook. Or you can use one of the strategies in the next chapter that will help you take your mind off of what is starting to annoy you. Over the next few weeks, when your body tells you are starting to feel upset, try using either the mindfulness exercise, a mantra, or a distraction technique described in the next chapter. See what helps you settle down the most.

Chapter 8: Calming activities that use emotional distraction

For most children and adults, when you get upset or angry it is very difficult to control your emotions. It doesn't usually work at that point to just tell yourself to calm down, to stop being so angry. This is, in part, because the emotional part of your brain is such a strong and central part that it can take over the more logical part of your brain. When you are angry, you will not usually be thinking about whether there is another way to look at the situation; rather you are more likely to blurt out your feelings.

Often, when people try to tell their brains to calm down, they actually become more frustrated and upset. This can turn into a negative spiral where you become even more frustrated with yourself for feeling angry. Has this ever happened to you?

With this in mind, you might be wondering, what should I be doing instead? While it is very challenging to use logical reasoning to change your thoughts and feelings, it is easier to choose activities that can have a direct impact on your emotions. The idea is to pick activities that you really like, activities that capture your attention and that you enjoy, so that your emotion changes from anger to feeling amused, happy, or joyful. Have you ever noticed that it is hard to feel angry if you are laughing or having a good time?

Changing your brain's focus is called emotional distraction. You pick an activity that will change your emotion away from anger. It has to be something you really like, that you really get into, in order for this strategy to work. Remember anger is a powerful emotion, so you have to substitute something else that has a powerful effect on you. This can be a very effective strategy for changing your frustration before you reach the point of exploding in rage. It works better the earlier you notice that you are getting angry. Once anger reaches the overload stage, it is harder to get yourself interested in a different activity.

Look back at worksheet #7 (entitled **High and Low Anger**) in chapter 6. You wrote down a couple of situations when your anger was at a low level. Write these examples down again in the worksheet below. Now read on for some choices for what you can do to distract your brain.

There are several activities that you can choose from for emotional distraction. Some change your emotion to pleasurable feelings, some change to a burst of physical energy, and some change to a feeling of peace and contentment. Try some of the activities below, or try one of your own, and see what works best for changing your emotions. Don't be discouraged if the activities do not work every time. But if they help you feel differently and avoid angry explosions some of the time, you are on track to developing better self-control.

The following strategies work best when you practice them for a week or two **before** trying them out during a stressful situation. When you are angry or in a stressful situation, it will be harder to think clearly and develop a plan. If you practice the skills when you are calm, they will become more automatic, and this will help you to be able to rely on them when you need them. Practice them by yourself, or together with your coach. Sometimes the activities are more fun and more distracting if you do them with someone, rather than by yourself.

Physical Activities: Many children and teens find that physical activities, like a sport or physical exercise, help them convert feelings of frustration into feelings of energy and accomplishment. When you exercise, your body releases "endorphins" and these chemicals improve your mood. Activities that get your heart rate up (for example, running, biking, or playing an active sport) are often the best for changing your mood from anger to physical energy and a feeling of release. Some people prefer activities that they can do alone (for example, running, swimming, or biking), and others prefer activities that they can do with a friend or family member (like kicking a soccer ball, or throwing a baseball, basketball, football, or rubber ball). We recommend you try out a couple options and see what works best for you!

In order to do a physical activity, you have to be in a place, like your home, where you have your equipment. Also, in most cases, it would need to be daytime, and the weather would have to be okay, because you would usually do these activities outside. Lastly, you need at least a half hour, if not longer, to really get a good workout. If you are in a situation (like at school) where you cannot use a physical activity, then read on for other activities you could choose.

"Chill" Activities: Many people find that "chill" activities—like listening to music, playing a favorite video game, watching television, video streaming, creative writing or drawing—help distract them from feeling down or angry, while also helping them feel relaxed and happy. The activities you choose should be things that you enjoy doing and that are not too frustrating. We don't recommend playing a video game that can make you feel angry when you are trying to feel happy or calm! Instead, choose something that helps you relax and that you know well.

These "chill" activities are available day or night, and you can get to them quickly if you get upset at home. If you are at school, you would not be able to use most of them. But you could talk with your teacher or counselor about some activity that you could use at school if you needed to calm down. Some students arrange with their teacher to go out to the water fountain or to the bathroom. One school made available to a student a small, empty room, and the child and his parents brought in a mat and a big rubber ball he could roll his body onto. Most schools would not have that extra space, but asking to leave the class and go for a short walk to the bathroom is often acceptable, especially if you work it out with the teacher in advance. Another possibility in school is to arrange with your teacher ahead of time to draw something or to read a book if you start feeling angry. Your parent might need to help explain to the teacher what you are working on, and why a break would be helpful.

Reaching Out: For many children and adults, reaching out to a friend or family member and talking about something *unrelated* can help to change their thoughts and feelings from anger into something different and positive. It's very important to be thoughtful when choosing whom you are going to reach out to. You want to talk to someone who will help you think about something happy and distract you from feeling angry, not someone who will criticize you or your emotions, or make you feel worse. If you are at school, you could arrange to go talk with your counselor, while if you were at home, you could talk with a family member, or use your phone to contact a friend.

Sensory Activities: Things that make you feel calm, cool, and relaxed physically often influence your mood. For some children and teens, this might involve wrapping yourself in a favorite furry blanket or smelling a scent that reminds you of a time when you felt happy and content. Other people find that changes in temperature can have a direct influence on their mood. If you often feel "hot" when you are angry, it may help you to hold an ice cube on your arm to cool off and calm down. Hold the ice cube as long as you can stand it. This may hurt a little but it will help get your mind off your anger. For these activities you would need to be at home, unless you were lucky and your school has an extra room for a blanket that you could use or where you could listen to your favorite music.

Using a Mantra: In chapter 5, we discussed how to use mantras (short, memorable sayings) to prevent anger from starting. We showed how mantras can be used before you face a frustrating situation, like when starting a difficult homework assignment or a test, or if you are around people who sometimes criticize or ignore you.

While previously you created mantras to help you before the frustrating situation even started, now we want you to try using these mantras if you are already in the midst of the frustrating situation. This can be a helpful tool to change your mood even when you have begun feeling angry. The trick is to catch it early because once you are increasingly angry, the mantras will be less effective.

Mantras work not only by shifting your attention but also by helping you look at a troubling situation in a new way. For example, if you are getting frustrated about having to fix mistakes in your homework, try to remind yourself that "everyone makes mistakes" or "when learning something new, we all make mistakes."

Read over the mantras you wrote down in chapter 5. If you haven't used them in a while, make sure that you practice the mantras while you are calm for a couple of weeks before you try using them in a stressful situation. Then when you start feeling angry, repeat one of the mantras in your head a number of times to calm down. Consider turning the mantra into a little song, and maybe it will make you smile or laugh. If you can smile or laugh, you are less likely to feel angry. The mantra may not stop your anger at first, but over time, it may lessen your anger so that you avoid an explosion. Keep practicing and congratulate yourself any time you don't blow up. The advantage of this activity is that it takes place in your head, so that you can do it anywhere.

Mindfulness: In chapter 7, we introduced a mindfulness exercise for when your body gave you a signal that you were upset. You can use this same exercise even if your body does not give you a signal. Mindfulness can help if you recognize that you are starting to get angry. Like many of the activities in this chapter it works better the earlier you realize you are getting angry.

Look over your anger diary from the beginning of the workbook and look over worksheet #7 that lists situations when your anger is sometimes at a lower level. These worksheets can give you clues about what situations to be on the lookout for. Before you use the mindfulness exercise to feel more at ease, try it out when you are relaxed for a few weeks. Then try it when you are starting to get upset. Does it help you feel a little bit calmer, more at peace? If so, add it to your "coping" toolbox below. Mindfulness gets easier with practice. Once you get good at it, you can do it in your head almost anywhere.

Another simple activity to try is a chime meditation. For this activity, a chime or bell is rung and you listen silently to the bell, focusing on the sound as it becomes quieter, and seeing when you can no longer hear the sound. You can repeat this and ring the bell three times to help your brain focus on the moment when you no longer hear the sound, and you might find yourself distracted from what has made you angry!

In summary: In order for an activity to work, it must change your emotional state. For each activity you try, think about how you felt before and afterwards. Did you feel differently after the activity? Try it a few times, because it takes practice to get better at it, and remember the goal is to help you reduce your angry outbursts, not necessarily to eliminate them altogether. So if a strategy works sometimes, keep it on your list.

It is ideal to have a few different strategies so you can choose the one that you feel like trying that day. You may find one strategy works better when you are full of energy, and another works better when you feel tired. You may be in the mood to be physically active some days, but prefer to talk or chill on others. Also, some activities you can only use at home, while others are useful no matter where you are. It is a good idea then to practice a few different strategies so that you can pick what might work better in a particular situation.

It is often helpful to discuss your strategies with an adult who is likely to be nearby at times that you tend to get angry. That way the adult could cue you if you forget to try your activity when you start to get angry. Sometimes you will find yourself focusing on what is irritating you and forget to use your strategies. This is when it can be helpful to have your coach or another adult remind you. However, the adult will only make the suggestion once. He could use a verbal or hand signal that you both had agreed on, and then it is up to you. There is no penalty for not listening to the signal. You decide.

Consider in advance what items you will need when you start to get angry. What will you want to use to distract you? If possible, gather what you will need ahead of time. For example, if you like to play ball, draw, watch a video, or wrap yourself in a blanket, make sure you have the items close by. If they are small enough, maybe have them in a corner of your room or in a box in the garage, so that you know where your materials are when you need them. This is not possible for bigger items, or for things you or your family use all the time, like a computer, television or phone.

Building my coping with anger toolbox: Worksheet # 9

Describe briefly two situations that get you angry. Refer back to your anger diary and to worksheet # 7 to remind yourself about what has triggered your anger in the past, or you could write about situations that made you frustrated or angry in the past week. For each situation circle or write in activities that you could use to distract yourself. For mantras or mindfulness exercises, remember to practice them for a couple of weeks when you are calm. Then try out your distracting activities when you start to get frustrated. After a month or so, put a darker circle around those activities that worked for you.

1. Describe one situation (or trigger) that is sometimes frustrating for you.
_____
_____

2. Which activities could you use to distract yourself? Circle or write down the ones you will try.

a) Physical activities, like running, biking, or playing a sport
_____

b) "Chill" activities, like music, video games, television or video streaming, creative writing, or drawing
_____

c) Reach out to a friend or family member, and talk about something unrelated to the anger arousing situation: Who is your "go to" person?
_____

d) Sensory activity, such as holding an ice cube on one's arm, or wrapping a furry blanket around one's body, or smelling something you like
_____

e) Using a mantra. What is your favorite mantra?
_____

f) Mindfulness exercise (like deep breathing or listening to the chime)
_____

g) Other
_____

Drs. David and Shira Gottlieb

3. Describe another situation that is sometimes frustrating for you.
_____
_____

4. Which activities could you use to distract yourself? Circle or write down the ones you will try.

a) Physical activities, like running, biking, or playing a sport
_____

b) "Chill" activities, like music, video games, television or video streaming, creative writing, or drawing
_____

c) Reach out to a friend or family member, and talk about something unrelated to the anger arousing situation: Who is your "go to" person?
_____

d) Sensory activity, such as holding an ice cube on one's arm, or wrapping a furry blanket around one's body, or smelling something you like
_____

e) Using a mantra. What is your favorite mantra?
_____

f) Mindfulness exercise (like deep breathing or listening to the chime)
_____

g) Other
_____

Remember in a few weeks to put a darker circle around those activities that worked well for you.

5. Creating a coping box:

a) What physical things (i.e. an iPod for music, a phone for contacting your friend, a soft blanket, a ball, drawing materials) do I need for my calming activities?
_____

b) Does it make sense to put them in a box in my room? Or else where will I find them?
_____

The Anger Overload Workbook

It is important to try out various activities the next few weeks and see what works for you, before going on to the next chapter.

Drs. David and Shira Gottlieb

Section 4: What to do for high levels of anger

Chapter 9: Picking a "go to place"

What if you haven't been able to catch your anger early and control it? What if you start exploding in anger: swearing, screaming, and/or throwing things? Later you will feel sorry for what you said and did, but you are not thinking rationally when you are in anger overload. So it is going to be real hard to stop yourself from hurting someone with your angry words or your angry actions.

You need to plan ahead in order to have a chance of slowing yourself down when you get extremely angry. Since you will not be thinking clearly then, you should pick a "go to place" ahead of time, a place where you can be alone when you get that mad. It is not usually possible to stop your anger when you are still looking at the person who made you mad. You are liable to keep letting him have it if you are together in the same room. So the key is to leave the scene as quickly as possible so that you do not continue to say or do things you will later regret.

Pick a place that you can get to quickly and that you find comforting when you are upset. Talk it over with your coach. Make sure it is a place that other people won't mind you using. For example, you may not be able to pick the family room as the "go to place" if other family members tend to hang out there. If other people are in the room, you will be tempted to continue debating with or screaming at them. If you have your own bedroom, that is often a good place to pick, because you can have privacy there and because you have things you can do there while you calm down. Some people like to lie down in their bed when they are angry, and some people play with a toy or use the computer.

Look back at your anger diary from the first three chapters. Where did you usually end up when you were extremely angry? Where did you tend to go, and what did you do there? It would make sense to go to that place when you get really upset in the future, since you have been comfortable using it in the past.

It can be more difficult to decide on a place if you get angry at school. There are not often private places you can go to in order to calm down. Talk with your teacher or counselor about what is possible. Maybe there is a waiting room near your counselor's office, or maybe you can go somewhere in the hall (near your locker), or maybe the bathroom. Make sure it is acceptable to your teacher, so that you can go there in the future if you get really upset. Ask if you can go there without waiting, since when you get mad, you want to leave the scene as quickly as possible. Some schools call this a "flash pass," a prearranged pass that allows you to leave immediately. If you wait, you are more likely to explode at someone in the class. Explain this to your teacher, and maybe have your parents, or your coach, help explain it to your teacher as well.

The other thing you want to tell your teacher, or whichever adult is usually nearby when you get angry, is not to try to talk you down. Talking about it does not usually work if someone is in anger overload. When you have calmed down somewhat then talking may help. If you are in the high anger stage, talking usually leads to an increase in angry feelings. But see what works for you. In most cases, a "go to place" away from others will be best. It may take some time to calm down, so make sure other people, like your teacher or parents, know that too.

Since you will be in anger overload and not thinking clearly, you may not think to go to the place you have chosen. Therefore, it is important to make a plan with someone who is usually nearby when you get mad, preferably not the person you usually get mad at. It would help if someone could cue you to go to the place you have chosen to calm down, if you forget to do so. The cue is best when it is short, nonverbal, and mutually agreed upon in advance. It could be putting up a hand, like a stop sign. Or it could be pointing in the direction you should go. Or it could be a few words like "Take five." Make sure it is something everyone knows about in advance. The reason it is best that the person you are angry with is not the one who will cue you is because you will be less likely to take his cue to heart, if you are mad at him. But sometimes that is the only other person there, and so hopefully you will listen to the cue and "take five" to unwind wherever you have chosen.

If you use the cue successfully to calm down, you would want to celebrate later with your coach. Celebrate with a fun activity in the house or in the neighborhood for ten to thirty minutes. You want to celebrate because it is really hard to stop screaming and go to the place you have chosen when you are that mad. So take a break later in the day and do something with your coach to reward yourself for making the effort to calm down.

My "go to place": Worksheet # 10

Where will you go at home to try to calm down?
_____

Do you need a place in school? If so, where?
_____

What is going to be the cue and who is going to give it?
_____

If you use the "go to place" when you are extremely angry, how will you celebrate?
_____

Drs. David and Shira Gottlieb

Chapter 10: Review and practice

Now it's time to put together a plan that takes into account all the work you have done in the previous chapters. Which strategies do you like? Which ones are more likely to work for you?

First, there are strategies for avoiding or altering situations so that you could prevent anger from even starting. One choice might be to stay away from people when they are crabby and more likely to make you angry. Another possibility could be to change the time you do something in order to avoid a conflict with someone else's agenda. You would still get to do what you want, but not at the exact time you wanted. Another alternative to prevent anger is to use a mantra before a difficult situation begins to help you look at things in a new way.

Then we looked at various strategies for when you experience low levels of anger. There are a number of possibilities that would change your emotion from anger to happiness or excitement. We call this emotional distraction, and the choices include physical activities, "chill" activities, sensory activities, reaching out to a family member or friend, using a mantra, and mindfulness exercises.

Finally, we reviewed your options for when you are extremely angry. Then your best bet usually is to have a "go to place" where you can wait until you calm down. If you don't leave the scene where you went into anger overload, you will probably say or do more things that you later regret. You could do any activity you want in your "go to place." The key is to wait until you are really calmer before you rejoin whoever made you mad.

On this next worksheet, pick out which strategies you want to use for several situations or triggers that you have been writing about in the previous worksheets of this workbook. Depending on the situation--who is with you, where you are, and what is bothering you--different strategies might work better than others. In the worksheet below, the various strategies are listed. Fill in the blanks for the strategies that you think will work best for you. After a few weeks, go back and put dark circles around the ones that have helped you.

For each situation, what are my strategies: Worksheet # 11

1) Describe one situation or trigger

_____

_____

Prevention strategies:

a) how to avoid it _____

b) how to alter the timing _____

c) a mantra I could use _____

Early anger phase:

a) any warning signals in your body_____

b) physical activities _____

c) chill activities _____

d) sensory activities _____

e) reaching out to someone _____

f) mantra(s)_____

g) mindfulness activity _____

High anger phase:

a) my "go to place" _____

b) What I like to do there _____

2) Describe another situation or trigger
_____
_____

Prevention strategies

a) how to avoid it _____

b) how to alter the timing _____

c) a mantra I could use _____

Early anger phase:

a) any warning signals in your body _____

b) physical activities _____

c) chill activities _____

d) sensory activities _____

e) reaching out to someone _____

f) mantra(s) _____

g) mindfulness activity _____

High anger phase:

a) my "go to place" _____

b) What I like to do there _____

3) Describe another situation or trigger
_____
_____

Prevention strategies:

a) how to avoid it _____

b) how to alter the timing _____

c) a mantra I could use _____

Early anger phase:

a) any warning signals in your body _____

b) physical activities _____

c) chill activities _____

d) sensory activities _____

e) reaching out to someone _____

f) mantra(s) _____

g) mindfulness activity _____

High anger phase:

a) my "go to place" _____

b) What I like to do there _____

Practice your choices for the next three weeks, and then circle the strategies that are working better for you.

Drs. David and Shira Gottlieb

Section 5: More advanced techniques

Chapter 11: How to deal with different points of view

Why do your mom or dad sometimes get annoyed with you? Why does your brother or sister interrupt you while you are trying to play a game or trying to talk on the phone with your friend? Why can't they just leave you alone?

These problems can occur because each person has different goals and worries. Goals are things we want to happen; they are things we work for. You can have a goal for one particular day or for a longer time, like for the coming year in school. For example, your goal for the day might be to spend time with a friend after school, while your goal for the school year could be to get a good grade in one or more of your classes, or to make a sports team at your school.

Your goals influence what you want to do with your time. If your goal is to be the pitcher for your baseball team, for example, you will want to practice pitching and maybe take some lessons on throwing a better fast ball. If your goal is to get to know your friends better, you will want to talk or text them more often. You can see how your goals affect what you plan to do. Think about your goals for this school year, and write down two of your goals in the worksheet below.

Your worries can also affect what you plan to do. Some worries are related to your goals. For example, if your goal is to get a good grade in math, you may get worried one night about an upcoming math test. If your goal is to be with your friends more often, then a related worry may be that you might not be invited to your friend's birthday party. Other worries may not be connected directly to your goals. Some of these worries could be about how you look: whether people will like your outfit or your shoes. Another worry could be whether your parents will take you to see a new movie that your friends have seen, or will your parents say no because they think the movie is too violent. Write down below a worry or two that you have had in the last few weeks.

Your goals and your worries affect what you do and what you think is important. Your parents' goals and worries may be different from yours. This difference can lead to tension and arguments. It may be why you could have a different opinion than your parent(s) do about what you should be doing after school, for example.

A difference in goals may also be why your brother or sister annoys you. For example, some day you may be on the phone with a friend, while your younger brother or sister keeps calling your name, or comes into your room. Your younger brother or sister may be lonely and want attention, while your goal is to get closer to your friends. The difference in goals can mean different opinions on how important it is for you to have privacy and not to be interrupted when you are on the phone with your friends.

Conflicts in goals can also occur between you and an older sibling. For example, your older brother or sister may want you to turn down your music because it is distracting while he is writing a paper for school. Your older sibling's point of view is that there should be quiet after school, while your point of view is that this is a good time to listen to music. So different goals can lead to different points of view, and different points of view can lead to conflict and arguments.

Here's a possible difference of opinion you could have with your parent(s). They may be worried about you doing well on an upcoming test, and may want you to get off the phone or skip practice for your sport after school. They may want you to come home and study for your test. Your parents have a different point of view because they are more worried about your test, while you are more concerned with talking with your friend or with getting to play on a sports team at school.

On the worksheet below where you wrote down a couple of your goals and worries, now add what you think one or two of your parents' goals and worries are for you. If you are not sure, ask them one night.

Goals and Worries: Worksheet # 12

Your goals this year:
1._____
2._____

Your recent worries:
1._____
2._____

Goal(s) or worries your parent(s) have for you:
_____
_____

How do their goals and worries compare to yours? How different are they? If they are different, you can expect that there will be disagreements sometimes with your parents on how you spend your time.

In the next chapter we will talk more about how to reach compromises with people who have different goals and worries. But for now, we want you to look back at your anger diary. Look for a couple disagreements with someone in your family or with someone at school, and on the next worksheet below, write down what happened. Were you wanting to do something that was different than what the other person wanted? Think about what the other person's goal or worry was. For each situation, write down below what your goal or worry was, and what you think the goal and worry was for the person with whom you were angry.

Drs. David and Shira Gottlieb

Now we are going to use this information to create a mantra to help you stay calmer the next time this situation, or a similar situation occurs again. The mantra can be something like "there is more than one way to look at this." This mantra can be used for most situations where there is an argument with another person.

You may prefer a mantra that is more specific, one that is written for a particular argument. An example for an argument about homework would be "Mom gets worried about my grades, that's why she gets on my case sometimes." An example for an argument with a sibling would be "my little brother probably wants some attention." Think about whether you would use one of these mantras for the situation you wrote about below, or whether you want to write one that fits better for your situation. Then write your choice for a mantra below. Choose a mantra or catch phrase that will help you keep in mind that there are different points of view.

The mantra won't settle the problem or prevent you from getting annoyed. But if you practice saying it to yourself, it will become easier to remember, and you may think of it when you are getting into an argument with your parents or siblings. It may keep you from exploding. If you remember at the time of the argument that they are worried or have a different goal, then you are less likely to feel they are uncaring or mean. They are not trying to be a pain in your butt! When you see a reason for their behavior, you probably won't get as mad.

Remind yourself of the mantra at least once a day for the next few weeks. If you do that, you are more likely to remember it at the time when the person is annoying you. The goal is for the mantra to become something you automatically think about when there is a difference of opinion. When you get annoyed, you are not going to be in the mood to search your brain for a possible mantra. That is why it is better to prepare in advance. You might even want to write the mantra down on a piece of paper in your room, or in your notebook, so that you will see it each day.

Ask your coach to write about a conflict when he had a difference of opinion with someone. He can use worksheet # 13 at the back of the book. What was his goal or worry, and how was it different from the person he was angry with? Then ask him what mantra he could use to remind himself of the difference in goals or worries.

Arguments based on different goals or worries: Worksheet # 13

Arguments you had with someone in your family or in your school:

Argument #1

_____
_____

What was your goal or worry?_____

What was the other person's goal or worry? _____

What is a possible mantra you could practice?
_____

Argument # 2
_____
_____

What was your goal or worry? _____

What was the other person's goal or worry? _____

What is a possible mantra you could practice?
_____

Drs. David and Shira Gottlieb

Chapter 12: How to compromise

One way to deal with a conflict when you have a different opinion than your parents, siblings, or friends is to search for a compromise. A compromise means you will not get to do everything you want. Sometimes you may get to do most of what you want, but not at the exact time you wanted. For example, you may get to go to a friend's house, but on the weekend, rather than after school. Sometimes you may have to change your plan to a different activity that is more acceptable to your family or friends. An example is that you may be allowed to have your friends come over, but not go to the mall with them. Remember that compromise means neither you nor the other person gets everything they wanted. But if you can come up with an idea that the other person can agree to, you will get to do some part of what you wanted.

Think about this: Is it better to get to do an important part of what you wanted, or argue about whether you should be allowed to do exactly what you want? Is the argument worth it? The problem with arguments is that often both people get so angry that nothing gets worked out, and then you don't get to do any part of what you wanted! Sometimes you even get punished for arguing too much.

Compromise is hard to do for several reasons. First, if what you want is important to you, it is hard to give up any part of it. We will consider an example in a moment, and you will see how hard it can be sometimes. Second, in order for a compromise to work, the other person must be in the mood to give up something too. Sometimes, the other person is either stubborn, or in a crabby mood, and will not consider compromising. The third reason it is difficult to reach a compromise is that when there is an argument everyone is usually pretty angry, and it is hard to think clearly about a possible compromise if either person is still angry.

Before you ask for something, try to anticipate whether there is likely to be a difference of opinion. Think about whether the other person said no to similar ideas in the past. If so, think about a possible compromise ahead of time, before you raise the issue. Consider also whether the other person is in a good mood or a crabby mood. Is this a good time to bring up your idea? Be prepared to be disappointed. Remember that despite your trying to think about someone else's opinions and about what the other person's mood is, the person may still say "no" to what you want to do. The other person may have such strong views that he may not be willing to compromise at all.

If an argument occurs, try to take a break and think some more about what each person's goals and worries are. Remember you will probably get nowhere if you keep talking when either of you is still angry. In the last chapter, we talked about goals and worries. Other people's goals and worries can cause their negative reaction to your plans. If the other person's goals and worries are very different from yours, then that person will likely have a different point of view from yours. But if you can figure out what the other person's goals and worries are, then you may be able to craft a compromise. Can you adjust what you want to do a little bit in order to put the other person at ease? If you can do that, the other person is more likely to say "yes".

Here's an example. Let's say a boy named Charlie is either watching a movie on television that his friend recommended or playing a game online with a friend. Charlie wants to finish the game or movie so that his friend will not be disappointed. Unfortunately, Charlie's parents yell that it is time to get ready for bed. Charlie does not want to stop. What could he do?

Charlie could try explaining why he wants to finish, but his parents will likely say that it doesn't matter, that he has to go to bed because he has school the next day. What are the parents' worries? They don't want Charlie to be tired in school the next day. Maybe they are also worried they will have a hard time waking Charlie up in the morning if he stays up late. On the other hand, Charlie is worried about disappointing his friend. In addition, he is probably enjoying the game or movie, and wants to finish. Are there any compromises possible here?

It won't be easy to think of a compromise in this situation because each person wants something done at precisely the same time. How can Charlie both finish the movie (or game), and at the same time get ready for bed? He can't split himself in two! One possibility that might satisfy his friend and his parents is to suggest to the parents that he take a few minutes to communicate online with his friend about why he has to stop playing the game, before turning off his computer. Charlie's parents may agree to five minutes because that won't throw off the time he gets to bed by much. In this case, the parents get most of what they want, and Charlie gets a little time to explain to his friend. His friend is not likely to be mad at him, because he knows how parents think! Charlie came up with an idea that took into account his own concerns about his friend and at the same time took into account his parents' worries.

Another conflict we have considered in previous chapters is when you and your parents have different ideas about what activity should be done right after school. You want to practice a sports activity in the backyard, for example, while your parents are worried about you finishing your homework and want you to get started right after you have a snack. They think you can practice the sport on the weekend. A compromise here that takes into account both opinions is to suggest a time limit for practicing after school, or to suggest that certain days you will practice, and other days you will get right to your homework. Each person gets part of what he wants. You could add that if you don't get your homework done on the days you practice, then you will give up some (or all) practice time for one week. Your parents then may be inclined to agree to this compromise, because you are in essence promising to get your work done, or else you will be giving up practice time in the week to come.

Now look back at the worksheet in the last chapter where you wrote about a situation when you had different worries or goals than someone in your family or school. Remind yourself what the issue was about, and on the worksheet below write two possible compromises. If you can't think of any, ask your coach for a suggestion. If you like his or her idea, you can write this in the space below.

If you are not sure what to write down, think it over for a couple of days. What is your main goal or worry? How can you accomplish what you want to do, and still satisfy what the other person is worried about? See if over the next couple of days you get an idea, and then write that below.

After you come up with one or two compromises, practice explaining the compromises out loud to your coach. See how your coach thinks it sounds. Be sure to keep a calm tone of voice, because if you are angry or sarcastic, the other person is less likely to accept your idea.

One way to start presenting a compromise is to put into words what each person's worry or goal is. If you can accurately explain what the person's worry or goal is, then that person will feel good. The person will think "yes, you understand me." When the other person feels understood, he is more likely to accept your proposal. Therefore, if you can, mention the other person's worries or goals as well as your own, and then present your compromise. We call this the "you feel…I feel…" compromise technique. Try it out with your coach, and ask him how it makes him feel.

Possible compromises: Worksheet # 14

Look back in the last chapter for worksheet # 13 about each person's goals and worries. Then write down possible compromises.

1) What was one argument in last chapter's worksheet?
_____

What was your goal or worry?
_____

What was the other person's goal or worry?
_____

What are possible compromises?

a._____
_____

b._____
_____

2) What was another argument about?
_____

What was your goal or worry?
_____

What was the other person's goal or worry?
_____

What are possible compromises?

a._____
_____

b._____
_____

Chapter 13: How to verbalize anger without losing self-control

Up to now the focus has not been on verbalizing your anger, but on preventing or altering your angry feelings. We have discussed a range of strategies: from anticipating problems and altering your plans and expectations, to using a mantra or an emotional distraction technique. The emphasis has been on maintaining self-control without expressing your anger directly to someone else. In the two last chapters, we also explained how to focus on goals and worries so that you can come up with a mantra or compromise and avoid a drawn out argument. These strategies are often effective in preventing anger overload.

As you get better at using the strategies we have outlined so far, you may now be in a position to sometimes directly verbalize your anger without going overboard. If you have been able to stop screaming, cursing, or throwing things, then you may be able to verbalize your anger while still maintaining self-control. This can be hard to do, but if you have been able to use the other strategies in this workbook so far, it is time to try verbal expression as another alternative. You will want to try this when it is important to let people know what is bothering you. But consider first how emotional you are feeling about the issue. If you are feeling aggravated before you start talking, then explaining how you feel may lead to an escalation that you later regret. Pick a time when you are pretty calm.

Verbal expression can be useful when the issue is something that you think will come up repeatedly, and you want the other person to keep in mind your feelings in the future. The other person may not change his opinion right away, but in the future he may be more sensitive to your wishes if you are able to express them in a clear way without losing self-control.

To do this, you must first have realistic expectations. It is unlikely you will change someone's mind right away. The other person may have strong opinions. Also keep in mind that people do not want to lose face, so they may not feel like agreeing with you right away, even if they are sympathetic to your issue. The idea is to let your feelings be known so that the other person will consider your feelings in the future. For example, if you like seeing your friends on Sundays, but your family is used to everyone being home for a family day, you might express your frustration in the hopes that eventually your family will realize that it is important for you to see your friends on some Sundays. You could add that it does not mean you have stopped loving or wanting to be with your family.

How could your verbalize this? You can use words like "annoyed," "frustrated," or "angry," but stay away from words like "hate," "awful," and "stupid." You want to say how you feel and tie your feelings to a specific issue, but not label the other person, or his ideas, with negative or hostile terms. For example, you could say "This is important to me. I get angry when you say I have to stay home every Sunday. I love you, but I also want sometimes to see my friends."

This is hard to do if you get extremely angry, but easier to do if you catch your anger at an earlier stage. Once you get to anger overload, you will not be thinking rationally and your emotions will come out in an extreme way. The time to verbalize your feelings then is before the issue gets into a hostile debate, or else wait until after you have calmed down. Some people find it easier to talk later in the day when they are calmer, rather than right away when they feel they might lose it.

Remember to speak about a specific problem, and don't put down the other person. In addition to tying your feelings to a specific issue, another approach is a variant of the compromise technique we wrote about in the last chapter. What you could do is say how you are feeling and also summarize how you think the other person is feeling. By recognizing the other person's feelings and thoughts, you are showing consideration and showing you have listened. The other person is more likely to show consideration for your feelings then.

Practice with your coach by picking an angry situation from your diary or a disagreement that occurred recently, and decide how you are going to verbalize your feelings. Use the worksheet below to outline your approach. Will you use the approach that shows your understanding for the other person's feelings, or do you prefer to focus on how to put your feelings into words, and leave out the other person's feelings? Either approach is fine. The key is to use a tone of voice that is clear and firm, but not sarcastic or critical toward the other person. You don't want the other person to feel put down, you just want him to understand why you want to do something.

Be sure to practice with your coach for a couple of weeks before you use this technique in an actual situation when you are angry. Ask your coach how you sound. Change roles and have your coach practice being you so that you can hear how your words sound. Do you feel the words are clear, but not sarcastic? After you have worked on your words and your tone, you can add this technique to your list of possible strategies.

Pick when to use it: when you are not close to anger overload already, and when some issue is likely to keep coming up (and you want the other person to consider your feelings in the future). Use your other strategies when you don't think talking about your feelings will be helpful, or when you are concerned you might lose it if you talk further. You may find that you get more angry the more you verbalize your feelings. If this approach doesn't work well for you, then don't use this strategy at all, and use the others in the workbook.

Remember that no matter what strategy you choose, you will not likely see the other person change his mind right away. Your goal is to influence his thinking in the future. You won't always get to do what you want, but you will find that your ideas are considered more often, compared to the past when you lost self-control.

Drs. David and Shira Gottlieb

Verbalizing your feelings: Worksheet # 15

1) What happened that got you angry?
_____

Describe your feelings _____
_____

Will you also explain the other person's feelings? If so, what will you say?
_____

2) Another situation when you got you angry
_____

Describe your feelings _____
_____

Will you also explain the other person's feelings? If so, what will you say?
_____

Section 6: Conclusion

Chapter 14: Ongoing review of anger plan

Now it is time to review your anger plan that you outlined in worksheet # 11 on pages 37 to 40. Make sure you put dark circles around the strategies that have helped you. There are empty spaces on that worksheet where you can add any of the advanced techniques from the last few chapters that you think may also help you with controlling your anger. If you read the section of the workbook about advanced techniques, look back over what you wrote down there. In chapter 11, did you find it helpful to think about other people's goals and worries? Or in chapter 12, did you come up with possible compromises? Or lastly, in chapter 13, did you practice verbalizing your feelings without losing your cool? If you found these strategies helpful, add them now to worksheet # 11 (on pages 37-40).

Only use the advanced techniques if you think they will help you. These tend to be more helpful for older children and teens than for younger children. Even for teens, you may feel that strategies, such as compromising, will not work in your situation. It may be too hard to find a compromise acceptable to everyone. You may also feel that talk of a compromise or trying to explain your feelings will lead to a heated argument. It may be better to avoid that possibility, then, and use one of the other techniques from earlier in the workbook.

For the next few months, on the weekends, look over your list of preferred techniques (see worksheet # 11). Make any adjustments based on what you found is still working and what, if anything, is not working. There may be some new conflicts that have come up, and you may find that other techniques are more helpful than the ones you have circled up to now.

Ask your coach for feedback, too. Would he recommend any changes in your strategies? It always helps to have an extra set of eyes. Sometimes you might overlook something that you are doing well, or you might need to tweak one of the strategies to make it more effective.

Once you are controlling your anger better, continue to review your list of strategies at the beginning of each month. As you get older, you will face new challenges and frustrations. Some of the strategies that you haven't used so far may become helpful.

The important message is that this is an ongoing process. Don't stop working on it now that you are finishing the workbook. Continue looking over your strategies and make whatever changes you think would help in the days and months to come.

Drs. David and Shira Gottlieb

Chapter 15: Summary

Learning to better control your anger is an ongoing process. Even most adults refine their techniques from time to time. Keep in mind too that no one is perfect. You may still experience anger overload sometimes. The goal is to reduce the number of times you lose it, so that you get people to respect you. You want people to listen to your feelings, and that is more likely to happen if you can refrain from swearing or throwing things when you get mad. You don't want people reacting negatively to your ideas because you lost control.

If you get stuck in one chapter, ask your coach for assistance, or skip that chapter for the time being. The workbook is intended to give you ideas about how you can control your anger. Different ideas are helpful for different people. Use the strategies that make the most sense to you. After you have finished the workbook, continue to review your strategies at the beginning of each month. Do you want to make any changes? Keep using the strategies that are working, drop those that are not working, and add any that you think might be helpful.

Keep practicing the strategies regularly. If you use a mantra for example, practice saying it to yourself each day so that you are more likely to remember it when you are beginning to get upset. Like practicing any new skill, it takes time and persistence. Ask your coach to practice with you, because many of the strategies involve interacting with another person. Keep in mind, too, that most of the strategies work best if you catch your anger early or if you can anticipate a problem and avoid it.

If you have worked on the exercises in this book and feel that you are still having trouble controlling your anger much of the time, consider asking your parents to look for professional help. Ask your parents to find a mental health professional in your area who knows about helping families with anger issues. A professional can determine if there are issues or events in your life that are contributing to your anger problems. Sometimes there are other problems in a person's life that make it difficult to control anger. If that is happening to you, then once you address the other issues, you will be able to more effectively utilize the strategies in this workbook.

You can learn to be the boss of your anger, rather than letting your anger be the boss of you! Your friends and family will listen to you and respect you. You won't get in trouble so much. Learning to control anger is not easy, but it is well worth the effort.

The Anger Overload Workbook

Appendix: Extra set of worksheets for your coach

My Anger Diary: Worksheet #1

1. The person you got angry at _____

What this person said or did that made you mad
_____
_____

What you said or did when you felt angry
_____
_____

After you got mad, where did you go until you felt better?
_____

What did you do until you felt better? _____

2. The person you got angry at _____

What this person said or did that made you mad
_____
_____

What you said or did when you felt angry
_____
_____

After you got mad, where did you go until you felt better?
_____

What did you do until you felt better? _____

3. The person you got angry at _____

What this person said or did that made you mad
_____
_____

Drs. David and Shira Gottlieb

What you said or did when you felt angry

_____
_____

After you got mad, where did you go until you felt better?

_____

What did you do until you felt better? _____

4. The person you got angry at _____

What this person said or did that made you mad

_____
_____

What you said or did when you felt angry

_____
_____

After you got mad, where did you go until you felt better?

_____

What did you do until you felt better? _____

5. The person you got angry at _____

What this person said or did that made you mad

_____
_____

What you said or did when you felt angry

_____
_____

After you got mad, where did you go until you felt better?

_____

What did you do until you felt better? _____

Looking for patterns: Worksheet #2

Are you usually mad at certain people? _____

And do you usually say certain words or do certain things when you get mad?
_____
_____

Lastly, where do you usually go and what do you do while you are calming down?
_____
_____

Drs. David and Shira Gottlieb

Identifying Who and What Gets You Mad: Worksheet #3

Now let's look more closely at the people and situations that get you angry. First look at whom you tend to get mad at. Circle any of the people below whom you have been angry with in the last few weeks.

A. People you get mad at:

1. Your mother
2. Your father
3. Your brother
4. Your sister
5. Your teacher
6. Your friend
7. Yourself
8. _____

Now look over your diary and think about what these people say or do that gets you mad. How do they sometimes frustrate you? Here are some choices that might fit for you, but if you see another pattern that fits better for you, then write that in the blank space below. Circle any of the triggers below that fit for your anger.

B. What these people said or did that got you mad:

1. They didn't let you do what you wanted.
2. They did something that was unfair.
3. They criticized you.
4. They ignored you.
5. They made you do something that you didn't want to do.
6. They interrupted what you were doing.
7. You got mad at yourself when you made a mistake.
8. _____

Pinning down what happened to you: Worksheet #4

Let's see if you can add more details to what it was that angered you. Below are some questions for each of the above triggers. Look for the number(s) of the triggers you just circled and then read the questions for those types of triggers below. Write in your answers in the spaces provided.

Look for the triggers you just circled in worksheet # 3:

#1 If they didn't let you do what you wanted:

    Is it usually an activity at home or out of the house? _____

    Do you want to play a game or use an electronic device? Or do you want to spend more time with friends? Or is it something else you want to do?
    _____

#2: If they were unfair:

    Which situation are they more likely to be unfair about:

        a) when you want to do something that your brothers, sisters, or friends are allowed to do, but you aren't, or

        b) when you want to do something else that you think is reasonable but they don't?

    What is it you want to do? _____

#3: If you were criticized:

    Are you criticized by friends or adults? _____

    Is it because of something they think you did wrong, or is someone picking on you because you are different in some way, like the way you dress or talk?
    _____

#4: If you felt ignored:

    Think about if there are certain times that this is more likely to happen: Is it at home or at school?
    _____

    If it is at home, is it usually after dinner, before bedtime, or when you ask for something? _____

If it is at school, is it in class, at free time, or at lunch?

___

#5: *If you were made to do things you did not want to do:*

Is the issue about chores, homework, getting ready for bed, or something else?

___

#6: *If they interrupted what you were doing:*

When is this more likely to happen: while you are on the computer, playing a game, watching television, or something else?

___

#7: *If you got mad at yourself when you made a mistake:*

Is it a mistake on schoolwork or homework, or does it have to do with an electronic game, a competitive sports game, or something else?

___

#8: *If it was a different trigger:*

What else are you doing when you get mad?

___

Now you are ready for the first strategy to help you be the boss of your anger.

The Anger Overload Workbook

Can you alter your routine? Worksheet #5

1. What is one trigger you noted in the previous chapter?
___

Can you avoid the person or the activity?
___

Can you change the time you do the activity?
___

Is there a good way to remind yourself to do something that will satisfy the other person?
___

2. What is another trigger you noted in the previous chapter?
___

Can you avoid the person or the activity?
___

Can you change the time you do the activity?
___

Is there a good way to remind yourself to do something that will satisfy the other person?
___

Drs. David and Shira Gottlieb

Coming up with a mantra: Worksheet # 6

What situation bothered you?
_____
_____

What is a mantra that could help you look at this situation in a new way?
_____

What's another situation that bothered you?
_____
_____

What is a mantra you could use?
_____

The Anger Overload Workbook

High and Low Anger: Worksheet # 7

What you do or say when **highly** angry:

1._____

2._____

3._____

Anything that has helped when you were in a high anger state?

_____
_____
_____

What you do or say when your anger is **low:**

1._____

2._____

3._____

Any ideas of what helped you control your anger?

_____
_____
_____

Drs. David and Shira Gottlieb

Knowing your body's signals: Worksheet # 8

What is one trigger for your anger?
_____

Are there any warning signs in your body? Circle any that apply to you, or write in one of your own.

a. Tightness or pain in your head, neck, back or shoulders
b. Stomach tightness, gurgling, or pain
c. Rapid breathing
d. Difficulty breathing
e. Heart beating faster
f. Other _____

What is another trigger for your anger? _____

Are there any warning signs in your body?
a. Tightness or pain in your head, neck, back or shoulders
b. Stomach tightness, gurgling, or pain
c. Rapid breathing
d. Difficulty breathing
e. Heart beating faster
f. Other _____

The Anger Overload Workbook

Building my coping with anger toolbox: Worksheet # 9

Describe briefly two situations that get you angry. Refer back to your anger diary and to worksheet # 7 to remind yourself about what has triggered your anger in the past, or you could write about situations that made you frustrated or angry in the past week. For each situation circle or write in activities that you could use to distract yourself. For mantras or mindfulness exercises, remember to practice them for a couple of weeks when you are calm. Then try out your distracting activities when you start to get frustrated. After a month or so, put a darker circle around those activities that worked for you.

1. Describe one situation (or trigger) that is sometimes frustrating for you.
_____
_____

2. Which activities could you use to distract yourself? Circle or write down the ones you will try.

a) Physical activities, like running, biking, or playing a sport
_____

b) "Chill" activities, like music, video games, television or video streaming, creative writing, or drawing
_____

c) Reach out to a friend or family member, and talk about something unrelated to the anger arousing situation: Who is your "go to" person?
_____

d) Sensory activity, such as holding an ice cube on one's arm, or wrapping a furry blanket around one's body, or smelling something you like
_____

e) Using a mantra. What is your favorite mantra?
_____

f) Mindfulness exercise (like deep breathing or listening to the chime)
_____

g) Other
_____

3. Describe another situation that is sometimes frustrating for you.
_____

Drs. David and Shira Gottlieb

4. Which activities could you use to distract yourself? Circle or write down the ones you will try.

a) Physical activities, like running, biking, or playing a sport

b) "Chill" activities, like music, video games, television or video streaming, creative writing, or drawing

c) Reach out to a friend or family member, and talk about something unrelated to the anger arousing situation: Who is your "go to" person?

d) Sensory activity, such as holding an ice cube on one's arm, or wrapping a furry blanket around one's body, or smelling something you like

e) Using a mantra. What is your favorite mantra?

f) Mindfulness exercise (like deep breathing or listening to the chime)

g) Other

Remember in a few weeks to put a darker circle around those activities that worked well for you.

5. Creating a coping box:

a) What physical things (i.e. an iPod for music, a phone for contacting your friend, a soft blanket, a ball, drawing materials) do I need for my calming activities?

b) Does it make sense to put them in a box in my room? Or else where will I find them?

My "go to place": Worksheet # 10

Where will you go at home to try to calm down?
_____

Do you need a place in school? If so, where?
_____

What is going to be the cue and who is going to give it?
_____

If you use the "go to place" when you are extremely angry, how will you celebrate?
_____

Drs. David and Shira Gottlieb

For each situation, what are my strategies: Worksheet # 11

1) Describe one situation or trigger
_____
_____

Prevention strategies:

a) how to avoid it _____

b) how to alter the timing _____

c) a mantra I could use _____

Early anger phase:

a) any warning signals in your body_____

b) physical activities _____

c) chill activities _____

d) sensory activities _____

e) reaching out to someone _____

f) mantra(s)_____

g) mindfulness activity _____

High anger phase:

a) my "go to place" _____

b) What I like to do there _____

2) Describe another situation or trigger
_____
_____

Prevention strategies

a) how to avoid it _____

b) how to alter the timing _____

c) a mantra I could use _____

Early anger phase:

a) any warning signals in your body _____

b) physical activities _____

c) chill activities _____

d) sensory activities _____

e) reaching out to someone _____

f) mantra(s) _____

g) mindfulness activity _____

High anger phase:

a) my "go to place" _____

b) What I like to do there _____

3) Describe another situation or trigger
_____
_____

Prevention strategies:

a) how to avoid it _____

b) how to alter the timing _____

c) a mantra I could use _____

Early anger phase:

a) any warning signals in your body_____

b) physical activities _____

c) chill activities _____

d) sensory activities _____

e) reaching out to someone _____

f) mantra(s)_____

g) mindfulness activity _____

High anger phase:

a) my "go to place" _____

b) What I like to do there _____

Goals and Worries: Worksheet # 12

Your goals this year:
1._____
2._____

Your recent worries:
1._____
2._____

Goal(s) or worries your parent(s) have for you:
_____
_____

Drs. David and Shira Gottlieb

Arguments based on different goals or worries: Worksheet # 13

Arguments you had with someone in your family or in your school:

Argument #1
_____
_____

What was your goal or worry?_____

What was the other person's goal or worry?_____

What is a possible mantra you could practice?
_____

Argument # 2
_____
_____

What was your goal or worry?_____

What was the other person's goal or worry?_____

What is a possible mantra you could practice?
_____

The Anger Overload Workbook

Possible compromises: Worksheet # 14

Look back in the last chapter for worksheet # 13 about each person's goals and worries. Then write down possible compromises.

1) What was one argument in last chapter's worksheet?
_____

What was your goal or worry?
_____

What was the other person's goal or worry?
_____

What are possible compromises?

a._____
_____

b._____
_____

2) What was another argument about?
_____

What was your goal or worry?
_____

What was the other person's goal or worry?
_____

What are possible compromises?

a._____
_____

b._____
_____

Drs. David and Shira Gottlieb

Verbalizing your feelings: Worksheet # 15

1) What happened that got you angry?
_____

Describe your feelings _____
_____

Will you also explain the other person's feelings? If so, what will you say?
_____

2) Another situation when you got you angry
_____

Describe your feelings _____
_____

Will you also explain the other person's feelings? If so, what will you say?
_____

Made in the USA
Lexington, KY
12 April 2016